HAL•LEONARD®

VIOLIN
PLAY-ALONG

AUDIO
ACCESS
INCLUDED

LINDSEY STIRLING
CHRISTMAS COLLECTION

T0084202

Jon Vriesacker, violin
Recorded and Produced by Jake Johnson
at Paradyme Productions

Speed • Pitch • Balance • Loop

To access audio visit:
www.halleonard.com/mylibrary

Enter Code
5849-0112-5826-9417

ISBN: 978-1-5400-5900-0

HAL•LEONARD®

Visit Hal Leonard Online at
www.halleonard.com

Contact us:
Hal Leonard
7777 West Bluemound Road
Milwaukee, WI 53213
Email: info@halleonard.com

In Europe, contact:
Hal Leonard Europe Limited
42 Wigmore Street
Marylebone, London, W1U 2RN
Email: info@halleonardeurope.com

In Australia, contact:
Hal Leonard Australia Pty. Ltd.
4 Lentara Court
Cheltenham, Victoria, 3192 Australia
Email: info@halleonard.com.au

Hallelujah

Words and Music by Leonard Cohen
Arranged by Lindsey Stirling

(There's No Place Like)
Home for the Holidays

Words and Music by Al Stillman and Robert Allen
Arranged by Lindsey Stirling

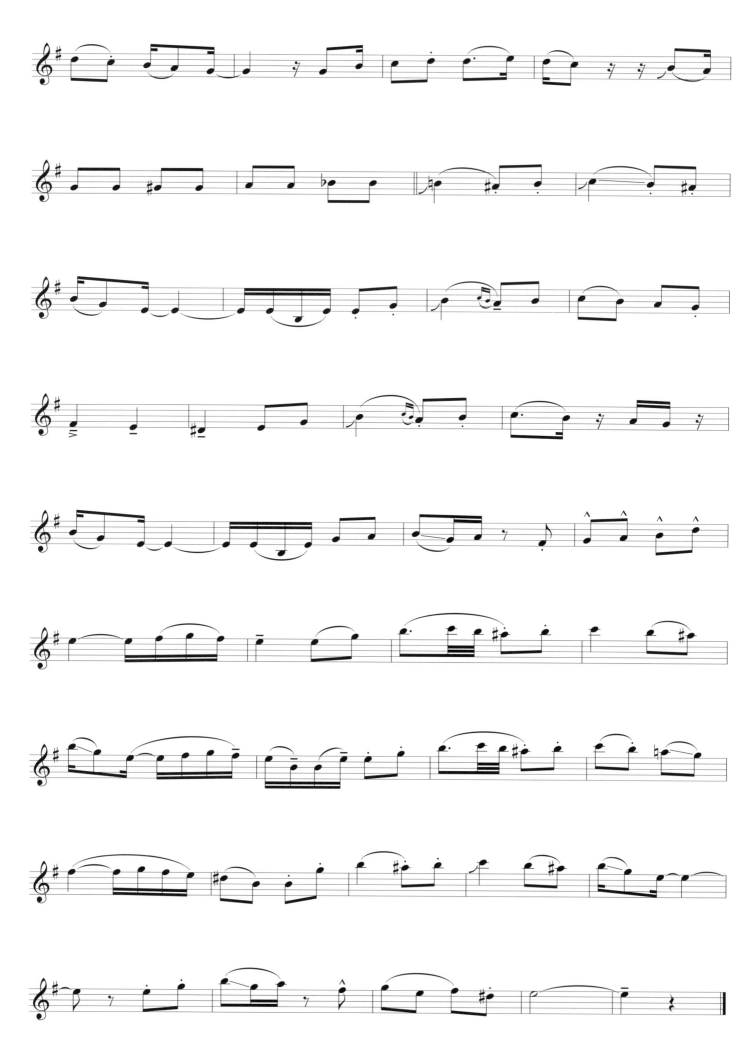

Dance of the Sugar Plum Fairy

from THE NUTCRACKER SUITE, OP. 71A

By Pyotr Il'yich Tchaikovsky

Arranged by Lindsey Stirling and Chris Walden

I Wonder as I Wander

By John Jacob Niles
Arranged by Lindsey Striling

*play cue notes on repeat

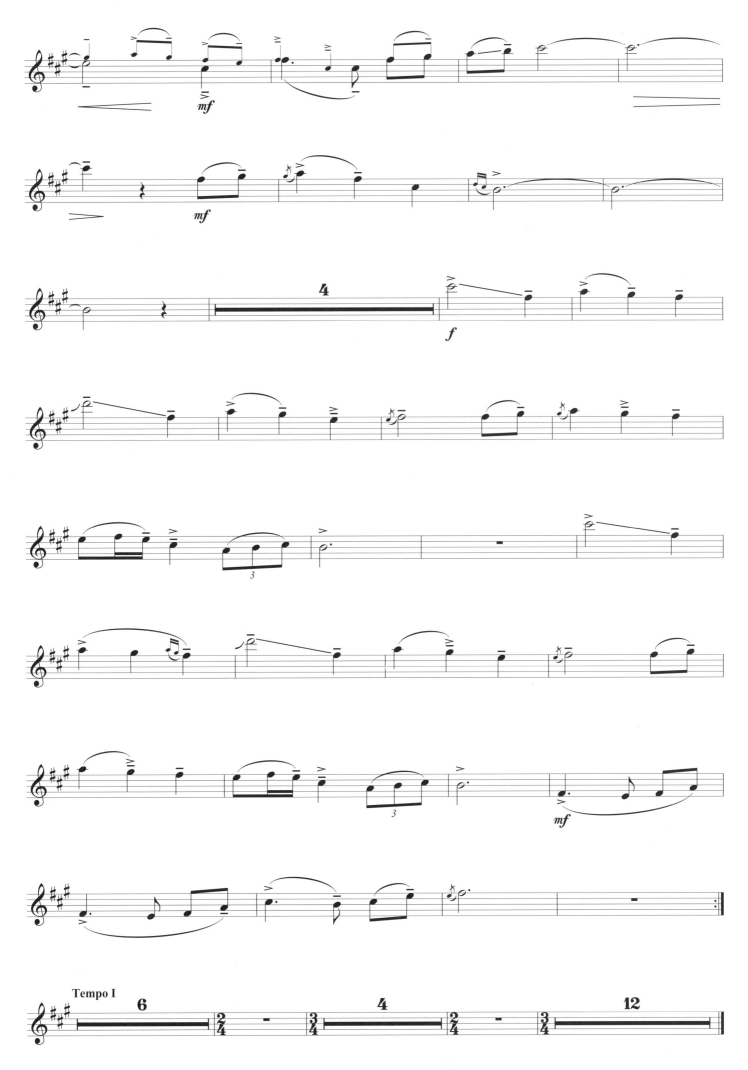

Shchedryk
(Carol of the Bells)

By Mykola Leontovych
Arranged by Lindsey Stirling and Ely Rise

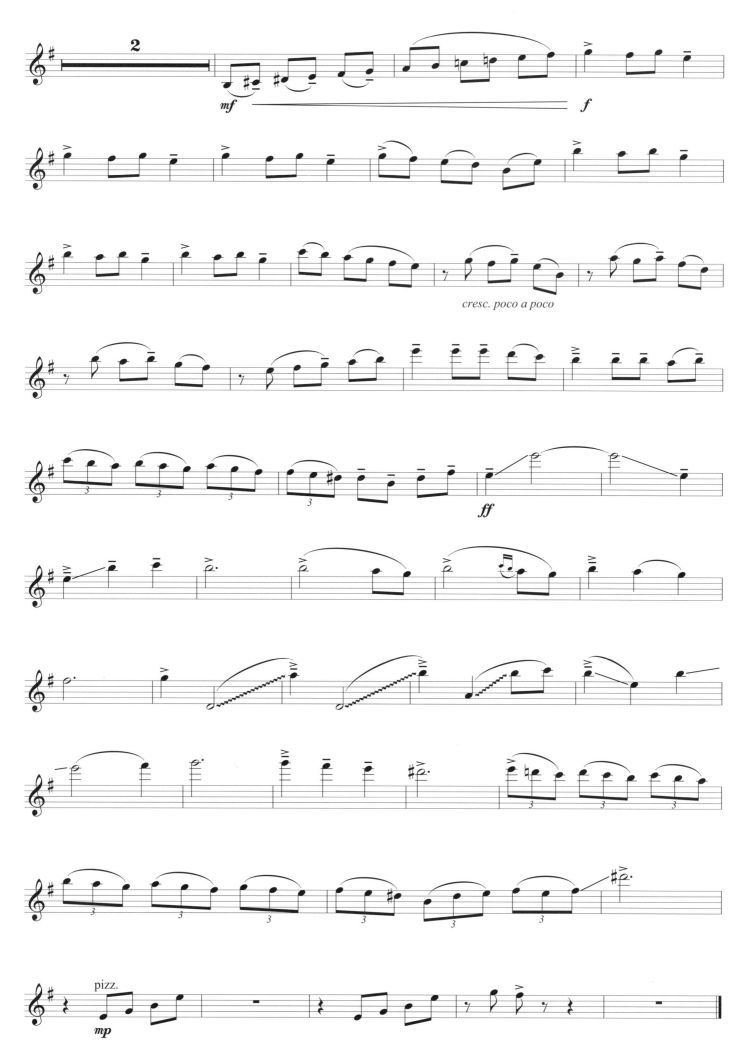

Mary, Did You Know?

Words and Music by Mark Lowry and Buddy Greene
Arranged by Lindsey Stirling

quoting Für Elise

Somewhere in My Memory

from the Twentieth Century Fox Motion Picture HOME ALONE
Words by Leslie Bricusse
Music by John Williams
Arranged by Lindsey Stirling

Santa Baby

By Joan Javits, Phil Springer and Tony Springer
Arranged by Lindsey Stirling

(There's No Place Like)
Home for the Holidays

Words and Music by Al Stillman and Robert Allen
Arranged by Lindsey Stirling

I Wonder as I Wander

By John Jacob Niles
Arranged by Lindsey Stirling

Santa Baby

By Joan Javits, Phil Springer and Tony Springer
Arranged by Lindsey Stirling